DUE   1/09

Johan Santana

By Jeffrey Zuehlke

AMAZING ATHLETES

Lerner Publications Company • Minneapolis

Copyright © 2007 by Lerner Publications Company

Lerner Publications Company
A division of Lerner Publishing Group
241 First Avenue North
Minneapolis, MN 55401 U.S.A.

Website address: www.lernerbooks.com

Zuehlke, Jeffrey, 1968–
    Johan Santana / by Jeffrey Zuehlke.
      p.   cm. — (Amazing athletes)
    Includes index.
    ISBN-13: 978-0-8225-6592-5 (lib. bdg. : alk. paper)
    ISBN-10: 0-8225-6592-7 (lib. bdg. : alk. paper)
    1. Santana, Johan. 2. Pitchers (Baseball)—Biography—Juvenile literature. I. Title.
GV865.S257Z84 2007
796.357092—dc22 [B]   2006022134

Manufactured in the United States of America
1 2 3 4 5 6 – DP – 12 11 10 09 08 07

TABLE OF CONTENTS

Johan fires a pitch during the September 10, 2006, game against the Detroit Tigers.

DOMINATING

Johan Santana stood tall on the **pitcher's mound**. Johan and his team, the Minnesota Twins, had to win this game. The Twins had been chasing the Detroit Tigers all summer for the **American League (AL) Central Division pennant**. The Twins were close to catching the Tigers. They needed a big game from Johan.

Johan leaned back and fired a blazing **fastball** toward home plate. The Tigers batter, Marcus Thames, swung hard and missed. The crowd of 40,000 Twins fans roared. A few pitches later, Johan zipped another fastball across the plate.

"Strike three!" shouted the umpire.

Magglio Ordóñez was up next. The Tigers right fielder is one of the AL's top power hitters. Could he get a hit against the Twins left-hander?

Johan's first pitch nicked the **strike zone.** "Strike one!" the umpire shouted. Two pitches later, Johan was ahead in the count—one ball, two strikes.

What would Johan throw next? His blazing 95-mile-per-hour fastball? Or his hard-breaking **slider**? Or what about his best pitch—the **changeup**?

Many people believe Johan has the best changeup in baseball. A changeup is a pitch that looks like a fastball. But it reaches the plate much more slowly. Hitters swing fast, thinking the ball is coming in hard. But they usually swing too soon and miss the ball.

Johan leaned back and threw. Ordóñez made a weak swing as the ball dropped toward the ground. A nasty changeup! Strike three!

Two batters later, Chris Shelton came up to the plate. Johan blew the Tigers first baseman away on four pitches. The last pitch was another wicked changeup. Shelton missed it by a mile. Johan had **struck out the side**!

The Twins were leading the game, 2–0. The team and their fans were confident. They had the best pitcher in baseball on the mound. Johan was leading **Major League Baseball (MLB)** in wins, strikeouts, and **earned run average (ERA)**.

Tigers shortstop Neifi Pérez led off the fifth inning. Johan struck him out with just three pitches! Next, Johan struck out catcher Vance Wilson on four pitches.

Johan struck out Neifi Pérez *(above)* of the Tigers.

Johan tips his hat to the crowd at the Metrodome in Minneapolis as he leaves the field during the seventh inning.

Finally, center fielder Brent Clevlen stepped into the batter's box. Johan's first pitch zipped over the plate. Strike one! Clevlen swung and missed badly for strike two.

The crowd stood and cheered. They wanted to see Johan strike out the side again!

The Twins pitcher launched the ball toward home plate. Clevlen swung. Suddenly, the ball dropped as it neared home plate. Another changeup! Clevlen swung and missed. The crowd erupted with joy as Johan jogged back to the dugout.

In the next few innings, the Twins piled on some runs. They won the game, 12–1. But afterward, no one was talking about Twins hitters. They were talking about Johan's 11 strikeouts. "He just dominates," said Twins third baseman Nick Punto. "That's why he's my MVP [most valuable player]."

Johan grew up in Tovar, Venezuela. His town is in the Andes Mountains of South America *(shown below)*.

SMALL TOWN BOY

Johan Alexander Santana was born on March 13, 1979, in Tovar, Venezuela. Venezuela lies on the northern tip of the continent of South America. Johan's hometown of Tovar is deep in the wild and green Andes Mountains.

Baseball is a very popular sport in Venezuela. Johan's father, Jesús, had played on his local team. But Jesús did not become a pro baseball player. Instead, he worked as an electrical engineer for the local power company.

Johan grew up in a family of five children. His older brother, Franklin, was a big, strong kid. Johan was a skinny bookworm. The family thought Johan would grow up to be an engineer like his father. But Johan loved baseball too. The young boy dreamed of being a shortstop like his dad. "I always wanted to be like him," Johan says.

Jesús Santana's skill as a fielder earned him the nickname the Octopus. He was so good at catching balls that it seemed as if he had eight arms.

Johan played baseball in Venezuela when he was young, just like these players.

Johan even grew up throwing right-handed, like his father. When he was 11, he went to a **tryout** for a local league. The coaches told him to try throwing left-handed. Johan quickly realized he could throw the ball much harder this way.

Johan's coaches had him play center field and first base. He was a good hitter, but his specialty was catching the ball. Johan loved to make diving catches in center field. He also loved to throw out runners with his powerful arm.

In 1994, 15-year-old Johan played in Venezuela's national championship series. Andres Reiner from the Houston Astros was there. He watched Johan make some great throws from center field. Reiner was impressed. He thought Johan had the talent to be a pro baseball player.

Reiner invited Johan to come to the Astros' baseball academy in Guacara, Venezuela. At first, Johan's parents weren't sure. Johan was young and still in high school. But Johan was excited to go. "Let me take my chance," he told his father.

Baseball is popular with young boys in Venezuela.

GOCHO

Johan joined the academy in January 1995. He was still just 15 years old. Students at the academy played baseball during the day. They studied English and other classwork in the evening. At first, Johan was terribly homesick. Guacara was a big city and very different from Johan's quiet hometown.

Other students made fun of Johan because

he came from a poor farming town. They called him Gocho. It is a Venezuelan slang word that refers to someone who lives out in the country.

After two months, Johan was ready to give up. But Andres Reiner convinced him to stick with it. In time, Johan got over feeling homesick and focused on baseball. Reiner talked Johan into trying pitching. The young left-hander quickly got the hang of it. His powerful arm could zip the ball over the plate at 95 miles per hour.

Johan also did well with his studies. "He was a bright student," said Reiner. "Our professor said he was the best student at learning English."

Johan isn't the only star player to come out of the Astros' Venezuelan baseball academy. Bobby Abreu of the Philadelphia Phillies and Melvin Mora of the Baltimore Orioles also learned many of their skills there.

In the summer of 1995, the Astros brought Johan to the United States. For the next four seasons, he pitched in the **minor**

Johan played for the Houston Astros for four years in the minor leagues.

leagues. If he continued to grow and learn, he would have a chance to play major league ball. Johan had lots of talent. But he wasn't always a winner. Sometimes he pitched well. Other times, he couldn't control where the ball was going. The Astros wondered if he was good enough to make it to the major leagues.

Other teams believed in Johan, though. In late 1999, the Twins arranged a trade to get him. They brought him up to the major leagues to see what he could do.

Johan pitches against the Kansas City Royals in 2000.

CHANGING UP

Johan spent the entire 2000 season with the Twins. He usually pitched as a **reliever.** He came in to pitch at the end of games. Johan struggled his first season. But he also showed promise. The Twins knew he had a lot of talent. They also saw that he worked hard and took his job seriously. Johan kept learning and getting better.

Twins manager Tom Kelly *(left)* removes Johan from a game in 2001.

In 2001, Johan got some **starts** for the Twins, pitching the first few innings of games. He also pitched as a reliever. He had a great fastball and a wicked slider. But most starting pitchers have three good pitches. The Twins wanted Johan to learn a third pitch.

For 2002, the Twins sent Johan back to the minor leagues. They wanted him to work on a third pitch—a changeup. Johan worked hard with his coaches. Soon he got the hang of the changeup. With that third pitch, minor league hitters had no chance against him. To start the season, Johan racked up an incredible 75 strikeouts in less than 50 innings.

The Twins called Johan back up to the majors. He pitched as a reliever for most of the season. But Johan still struggled with his **control.** He didn't always throw the ball to the spot he wanted. But when he pitched well, Johan was almost unbeatable. Even though he had spent part of the year in the minors, he still led the Twins with 137 strikeouts. He helped the team make it to the **playoffs.**

Johan pitches for the Twins in 2002.

Johan hoped to begin the 2003 season in the Twins' **starting rotation.** But manager Ron Gardenhire wanted Johan to stay in the **bullpen.**

Ron Gardenhire, Twins manager since 2002, put Johan in the bullpen for the beginning of the 2003 season.

Gardenhire felt his young pitcher needed to continue to work and get better. Johan was furious. He thought he deserved a chance to start.

Johan took out his anger on American League hitters. He didn't allow a run in his first seven games. He racked up dozens of strikeouts. He pitched so well that the Twins decided to make him a starter.

Johan soon proved he was the team's **ace.** He finished the season with 12 wins and 3 losses. He had an excellent 3.07 ERA. The Twins made it to the playoffs again. Johan faced the mighty New York Yankees in the 2003 **Division Series.** He pitched great but had to leave the game with an injury. The Twins ended up losing to the Yankees. But for Johan, the best was yet to come.

Johan has an unusual way of getting ready to pitch. He plays a baseball video game on his PlayStation Portable.

Johan faces the Baltimore Orioles in September 2004.

Ace

The 2004 season started out poorly for Johan. He had a sore elbow and didn't pitch well. But by June, he was back on track.

Johan started July with 7 wins and 6 losses. For the rest of the season, he didn't lose a single game. In fact, he won 13 straight. He blew hitters away with his three great pitches. His 265 strikeouts were the most by any American League pitcher. Teams struggled to score a single run off him.

Johan even made great plays in the field. He snatched hard line drives out of midair. He dove off the mound to make catches.

With Johan, the Twins easily made the playoffs again. They faced the great New York Yankees in the 2004 Division Series. Johan started and led his team to a win in Game 1. But the Yankees came back to win the series.

After the playoffs ended, Johan received some fantastic news. He had won the American League Cy Young Award! This award goes to the best pitcher in each league for that season. "This is

Johan holds up the 2004 Cy Young Award trophy for fans at the Metrodome.

Fans in Venezuela celebrate after Johan won the Cy Young Award in 2004.

like a dream come true," said Johan when he heard the news.

Millions of people in Venezuela celebrated. The young Gocho had become a national hero. The president of Venezuela invited Johan to his home to celebrate. "Gochomania" swept the nation.

Johan and his wife, Yasmile *(left)*, and their daughters, Jasmily and Jasmine, in 2005.

Before the 2005 season, Johan signed a **contract** to play for the Twins for four more years. The Twins agreed to pay him $40 million! He was rich beyond his wildest dreams. He built a big home in Fort Myers, Florida. He lives there during the **off-season** with his wife, Yasmile, and his two daughters, Jasmily and Jasmine.

Johan had another great season in 2005. But the Twins struggled to score runs. They failed to make the playoffs.

The Twins had a slow start to the 2006 season. By June, they had a losing record and seemed out of the playoff picture.

But then Johan and his teammates got hot. With Johan leading the way, the Twins had the best record in baseball in the second half of the season. Johan racked up an amazing 19 wins. He led MLB in strikeouts and ERA. "Johan is the best pitcher we faced this season," said Kansas City Royals slugger Mike Sweeney.

The Twins rolled into the playoffs. The team and their fans had huge hopes for a World Series win. But the Oakland A's shocked everyone by beating Minnesota in the division series.

The loss was tough to take, but Johan received some good news a few weeks later. He had won the 2006 AL Cy Young Award!

Meanwhile, Gochomania continues. All of Johan's starts are shown on Venezuelan TV. Venezuelans living in the United States go to Twins games to cheer their hero. "It's always good to make a lot of people happy," Johan says. "There's nothing better than that."

Johan gets ready to throw a pitch during the first game of the American League Division Series against the Oakland Athletics.

Selected Career Highlights

2006 Won American League Cy Young Award
     for second time
Won 19 games, tying Chien-Ming Wang
     of the New York Yankees for first place
     in MLB
Led MLB with a 2.77 ERA
Led MLB in strikeouts with 245
Finished fourth in Major League Baseball
     in innings pitched with 233.2

2005 Became first Minnesota Twin to lead
     major leagues in strikeouts with 238
Finished second in the American League in innings pitched with
     236⅔
Won 16 games and lost 7 with a 2.87 ERA
Struck out a career-high 14 hitters in a game against the Cleveland
     Indians

2004 Won American League Cy Young Award by unanimous vote
Won 20 games and lost 6 with a 2.61 ERA
Led American League in strikeouts with 265
Finished second in the American League in innings pitched with 228
Named American League Pitcher of the Month for July, August, and
     September

2003 Won 12 games and lost 3 with a 3.07 ERA
Struck out 169 batters in 158⅓ innings
Appeared in 45 games, including 18 starts

2002 Struck out 137 batters in 108⅓ innnings
Won 8 games and lost 6 with a 2.99 ERA
Pitched in 27 games, including 14 starts

2001 Struck out 28 batters in 43⅔ innings
Pitched in 15 games, including 4 starts

2000 Struck out 64 batters in 86 innings
Appeared in 30 games, including 5 starts
Pitched in his first major-league game for the Minnesota Twins on
     April 3

Glossary

ace: a team's top starting pitcher

American League (AL): one of MLB's two leagues. The American League has 14 teams, including the Minnesota Twins, New York Yankees, Boston Red Sox, Detroit Tigers, Chicago White Sox, and others.

bullpen: a team's group of relief pitchers

Central Division: one of the three groups that make up the American League. The AL Central is made up of the Chicago White Sox, Cleveland Indians, Detroit Tigers, Kansas City Royals, and Minnesota Twins.

changeup: a pitch that looks like a fastball coming out of the pitcher's hand but arrives much more slowly

contract: a written agreement between a player and a team

control: a pitcher's ability to throw the ball where he wants it to go

Division Series: the first round of Major League Baseball's playoffs. Teams play a five-game series. The first team to win three games moves on to the League Championship Series.

earned run average (ERA): a statistic that shows how many runs a pitcher has allowed per nine innings pitched. For example, if a pitcher pitches nine innings and gives up three runs, the pitcher's ERA would be 3.00.

fastball: a fast pitch that usually travels straight

Major League Baseball (MLB): the top group of professional men's baseball teams in North America. The MLB is divided into the National League and the American League.

minor leagues: groups of teams in which players improve their skills and prepare to move to the majors

off-season: the time between seasons of baseball

pennant: the division championship. In baseball, the team with the most wins in its division during the season wins the pennant.

pitcher's mound: the hill in the center of the baseball diamond where the pitcher stands when pitching

playoffs: a series of games played after the regular season to determine a championship

reliever: a pitcher who comes into a game after it has already started

slider: a hard, fast pitch that breaks, or curves, as it nears the plate

starting rotation: the group of pitchers—usually five—who start most of a team's games

starts: assignments to be the first pitcher of a game

strike zone: an imaginary rectangle over home plate. Pitches that pass through the rectangle are strikes. Pitches outside the lines of the rectangle are balls.

struck out the side: to have gotten all three outs in an inning with strikeouts

tryout: an event in which players are invited to show their skills to coaches

Further Reading & Websites

Geng, Don. *Beginning Baseball.* Minneapolis: Lerner Publications Company, 1995.

Geng, Don. *Play-by-Play Baseball.* Minneapolis: LernerSports, 2001.

Jones, Helga. *Venezuela.* Minneapolis: Lerner Publications Company, 2000.

Kelley, James. *Baseball.* New York: DK Publishing, 2005.

Minnesota Twins: The Official Site
http://minnesota.twins.mlb.com/
The Minnesota Twins official site has all the latest news about the Twins and Johan Santana.

Official MLB site
http://www.mlb.com
The official site of Major League Baseball provides up-to-date news and statistics of all 30 major-league teams and every major-league player.

Sports Illustrated for Kids
http://www.sikids.com
The *Sports Illustrated for Kids* website covers all sports, including baseball.

Index

Photo Acknowledgments

The images in this book are used with the permission of: © Bruce
Kluckhohn, p. 4; © AP Images/Paul Battaglia, pp. 7, 8; © Gabriela
Medina/SuperStock, p. 10; © Macduff Everton/CORBIS, p. 12; © Getty
Images, pp. 14, 17, 18, 19, 20, 22, 24, 28, 29; © AP Images/David Maris, p. 25.

Front Cover: © Bruce Kluckhohn